MARDI GRAS

D1310784

CARNIVAL NIGHT. THE PROCESSION.

The recently organized Krewe of Proteus had for the subject of its second parade on February 5, 1883, "The History of France." The krewe's costumes along with the outfits of Momus and Rex were on the steamer Dryburgh Abbey en route from France. When the ship was delayed by bad weather, the parade was costumed with what the krewe could scrape together in New Orleans. Shown is the title car, from Harper's Illustrated Weekly, *February 24, 1883.*

MARDI GRAS

A Pictorial History
of Carnival in New Orleans

By LEONARD V. HUBER

PELICAN PUBLISHING COMPANY
Gretna 2003

NEW HANOVER COUNTY
PUBLIC LIBRARY
201 CHESTNUT STREET
WILMINGTON, NC 28401

Copyright © 1977
By Leonard V. Huber
All rights reserved

Second printing, November 1989
Third printing, January 1994
Fourth printing, October 2003

Library of Congress Cataloging in Publication Data

Huber, Leonard Victor, 1903–
   Mardi Gras: a pictorial history of Carnival in New Orleans.

   1. New Orleans—Carnival—Pictorial works.

I. Title.
GT4211.N4H82   394.2'5'0976335   76-39911
ISBN 0–88289–160–X

Printed in the United States of America

Published by Pelican Publishing Company, Inc.
1000 Burmaster Street, Gretna, Louisiana 70053

Designed by Gerald Bower

MARDI GRAS

Starting just after Christmas and continuing until Lent, the carnival season in New Orleans, Louisiana, is observed with some ninety large-scale tableau balls and more than fifty street parades, culminating in the elaborate Rex pageant on Mardi Gras (Fat Tuesday), or Shrove Tuesday. About half a million people, natives as well as visitors, line the streets of the city along the parade routes. More than fifty thousand of them are in costume, and from sunup to sundown they may wear masks. These and the organized marching clubs, the colorfully decorated trucks carrying musicians and jolly costumed people, all participate in the revelry over which Rex, King of Carnival, presides.

Nearly two decades before New Orleans was founded in 1718, Mardi Gras had become part of the local geography, for it was on that holiday in 1699 that Iberville rediscovered the Mississippi River and camped for the night on the bank of a little bayou that he appropriately named Bayou du Mardi Gras—the first place-name in Louisiana.

Early in the city's history, the French settlers celebrated Mardi Gras in one fashion or another. When Governor William C. C. Claiborne inaugurated the American regime in New Orleans in 1803, he was impressed by the passionate love of the Creole population for dancing and holding masked balls. During the early years of the nineteenth century, the Crescent City's reputation as a gay, carefree town was enhanced. Public ballrooms, such as John Davis' adjoining the Théâtre d'Orléans, were the scenes of a continual round of subscription and masked balls when these were permitted by the authorities. As early as 1837 the first organized masquerade parade in carriages took to the streets and was followed by a delighted crowd of onlookers. Before that, there had been some street masking on Mardi Gras and even some organized groups such as the Beduin Company. In the 1840s more and more maskers thronged the streets on Mardi Gras, some on foot and the better heeled in carriages and wagons, and many of the masqueraders in carriages tossed bonbons and *dragées* (sugarcoated almonds) for extra fun. They also tossed little bags of flour, which broke upon striking a person, showering him with a coating of white. But onlookers also armed themselves with bags of flour, tossing them at the maskers, and one writer described certain streets in New Orleans on Ash Wednesday as presenting the aspect of a snow blanket. Moreover, the street rowdies who followed the masqueraders began to toss dust and even quicklime, and soon the local press was clamoring for an end to the celebrations. In 1854 the *Bee* reported on the festivities of the day before: "Boys with bags of flour paraded the streets, and painted Jezabels exhibited themselves in public carriages, and that is about all. We are not sorry that this miserable annual exhibition is rapidly becoming extinct. It originated in a barbarous age and is worthy of only such." But the gloomy predictions of the *Bee* did not come to pass, and today maskers still toss trinkets from floats. Unfortunately, the throwing of objects at masqueraders continues too but, instead of flour, dust, and lime, the rowdies throw small objects and even occasionally a brick or bottle. By the middle 1850s, though the balls continued to flourish, rowdyism on the streets had so invaded Mardi Gras that the New Orleans press clamored for the abandonment of a once-merry festival that "had become vulgar, tasteless and spiritless."

New Orleans was changing, growing in size and wealth. Though bringing customs and religion that were alien to the Creoles, the newcomers readily adapted themselves to the Gallic spirit that permeated the social life of New Orleans. One of the great contradictions, in a city of contradictions, is the fact that six Anglo-Saxons from nearby Mobile, Alabama, saved the great Latin festival of carnival for New Orleans and gave to this world-famous celebration its present form. By bringing imagination and organization into play, the Americans developed Mardi Gras into an institution of fantasy that the "Creole soon acknowledged with pride and in which his spirit and genius have remained predominant."

The Mystick Krewe of Comus, the first formal New Orleans carnival organization, sprang almost full-blown from the minds of the six young men who had been members of a carnival group in Mobile, the Cowbellians, formed about 1831. They chose a minor Greek god of festive mirth as their patron, and the young organization soon had eighty-three members, most of whom bore Anglo-Saxon names. All members were pledged to secrecy. By dint of prodigious labor (and considerable help from the Cowbellians), Comus and his cohorts presented on Mardi Gras night, February 24, 1857, a torchlight parade with the theme "The Demon Actors in Milton's *Paradise Lost*." All characters were on foot except Comus and Satan, who rode on decorated floats. After the parade, the krewe repaired to the Gaiety Theatre for a tableau ball.

Encouraged by the enthusiastic reception given their first efforts, Comus and his krewe produced an even better parade the next year, "The Classic Pantheon," with thirty-one floats on which rode maskers dressed to represent such characters as Jupiter, Minerva, Apollo, Janus, Ceres, Flora, Pan, and Bacchus. This pageant, which reportedly cost the members twenty thousand dollars, was described as one of "taste, brilliancy and beauty." Even the far-off *Illustrated London News* ran a woodcut and a description of it on May 8, 1858.

> *N. O., Jan. 4, 1857.*
> *You are requested to meet a few of your friends at the "Club Room" over the Gem, Royal street, on Saturday evening, the 10 inst., at 7 o'clock.*
>
> | | |
> |---|---|
> | S. M. TODD, | F. SHAW, JR. |
> | L D. ADDISON, | JOS. ELLISON. |
> | J. H. POPE, | WM. P. ELLISON. |

This little card inviting "a few of your friends" was sent in January, 1857, by six ex-Mobilians living in New Orleans for the purpose of forming what was to be the first carnival organization in the Crescent City. All six who signed the card bore Anglo-Saxon names.

The Gem Café, on Royal Street near Canal, was in its day a gathering place for the elite young men of the city. It was also the birthplace of the New Orleans carnival as we know it today, for it was here that the Mystick Krewe of Comus was organized.

By 1861 Comus' pageants and glittering tableau balls had firmly become part of the local scene, but the Civil War temporarily ended the Mardi Gras festivities. In 1862 New Orleans fell to David Farragut, and it was not until 1866 that Comus returned once more with a street parade and ball having the subject "The Past, the Present, and the Future," depicting the "Horrors and Sorrows of War," the "Blessings and Beauties of Peace," and the "Hope of a Smiling Future."

In 1867 the Mystick Krewe of Comus produced one of its most extraordinary creations, "The Triumph of Epicurus," in which the entire cast paraded on foot wearing papier-mâché disguises representing an elaborate banquet. Led by Le Gourmand, this grotesque assemblage delighted the thousands of spectators with representations of raw oysters, shrimp, huge bowls of soup, fish, vegetables, game, the traditional *boeuf gras* (the fatted ox symbolizing the last meat eaten before the Lenten fast), the accompanying wines, coffee, dessert and cigars, and the necessary knives, forks, and spoons—even candelabra. There were eighty-five figures in all.

The early 1870s saw an increase in carnival organizations. The Lord of Misrule, King of the Twelfth Night Revelers, made his bow on the streets in 1870 with a parade and tableau at the French Opera House that featured an immense Twelfth Night cake surrounded by the court of *Roi de la Fève.*

The second Comus parade, Mardi Gras, 1858, at the corner of Canal and Royal streets. From the London Illustrated News, *May 8, 1858.*

In 1867 Comus staged one of its most extraordinary creations, "The Triumph of Epicurus; or, The Gourmand's Vision." The entire cast of eighty-five marched on foot in papier-mâché disguises which represented all the elements of a three-course dinner with everything from soup to Kirsch and Curaçao. The krewe paraded in a cold drizzle, but thousands braved the bad weather to witness this parade. This engraving shows the parade passing on St. Charles Avenue near Poydras Street. The St. Charles and Academy of Music theaters, the Olympic Music Hall, and Strong's Saloon are now but memories. From Frank Leslie's Illustrated Weekly, 1867.

After Comus' parade, "The Missing Links to Darwin's Origin of Species," a satire on Darwinian theory and carpetbag rule, the krewe staged two tableaux at the Varieties Theatre. The one illustrated shows the gorilla crowning himself king with Chacma (the baboon) as his queen and two butterflies dancing to the music of the beetle fiddler, who is accompanied by anvil music played by the moth. Comus (foreground), goblet in hand, stands unawed and unabashed before the gorilla and the animals who kneel in subjection. From Harper's Illustrated Weekly, March 29, 1873.

During the bitter Reconstruction period, there were three parades with themes satirizing contemporary politics. The first of these was put on by the Twelfth Night Revelers in 1873, with the subject ''The World of Audubon.'' It is described by Perry Young in *Carnival and Mardi Gras:*

> Men of a generation just past remembered those costumes and tableaux as one of the marvels in carnival history, but each of the cars bore reference, too veiled for our day to understand, to the rulers of state and city. First car was an immense Twelfth Night Cake, next Audubon and his servants,

For many years carnival balls were held in the French Opera House, which burned in 1919. Although photographs of the interior of this building exist, only one or two sketches of the balls themselves are known. This one, by C. E. H. Bonwill, is from Frank Leslie's Illustrated Newspaper *and depicts a costume ball given on Washington's Birthday in 1864 by Mrs. Nathaniel Banks, wife of the Union commander in occupied New Orleans.*

the third a Parrot teaching school, pointing to "B" for Bugbear Butler. Car five showed the Fox (carpetbagger) addressing the Barnyard, car six the White Dove and Ground Dove holily united in matrimony by Cardinal Grosbeak. Car fifteen was "The Crows in Council", a travesty on the Louisiana State Legislature, in the State House, including the Carrion Crow with carpetbag in hand, bayonets protecting their seats. (This was called the "Bayonet Legislature" after federal arms had ousted all its Democrats.) On car seventeen was Pelican, the state bird, trying to hold her young to the nest and keep them fed.

In 1873 Comus presented "The Missing Link to Darwin's *Origin of Species,*" which satirized Darwin, the Republican party in Louisiana and in the nation, and the New Orleans Metropolitan Police, which kept the Radicals in power. Except for two cars, the entire krewe marched disguised in great papier-mâché masks, representing crustaceans, fishes, reptiles, insects, rodents, ruminants, carnivores, and quadrumana. The parade was described in a clever poem that was painted on transparencies carried along with it. Not all masks were satires, although they appeared frequently. Among the easily recognized characters were President U. S. Grant, the tobacco grub; the hated General Benjamin ("Spoons") Butler—whose occupation of New Orleans with federal troops in 1862 was then still fresh in mind—the hyena; the rabble-rousing R. J. Pitkin, "the cunning fox which joins the coon"; and Governor Henry Clay Warmoth, the serpent, "author of all our Woes." This parade, led by the despised Metropolitans (and the police still lead parades today), was blocked by a crowd of jeering, defiant men at Canal Street. The krewe thereupon turned back with their ineffectual escort and entered the Varieties Theatre for the ball, leaving some ten thousand spectators on the downtown side of Canal Street waiting in disappointment.

The floats of this particular Comus parade were the first to be constructed in New Orleans. Previously, the big masks and animal figures had been made in France, but by 1873 local artisans were able to make them stronger and no doubt cheaper. A new industry was born.

In January, 1872, another organization came into being, one destined to have the greatest influence on the yearly celebration of Mardi Gras. Rex was the creation of a group of men led by Colonel Walter Merriam, "a man of culture, taste, liberality and public spirit," who was also the proprietor of the Crescent Billiard Hall, and Edward C. Hancock, the assistant editor of the New Orleans *Times.* They conceived the idea of forming a grand procession on Mardi Gras of the heretofore unorganized maskers, carriages, wagons, etc., under the command of the King of

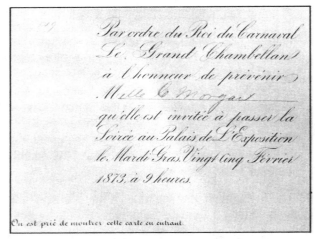

An invitation, in French, to the first Rex ball in 1873.

The Grand Duke Alexis of Russia, whose visit to New Orleans on Mardi Gras inspired the businessmen to form the Rex organization.

The parade of Comus passing the City Hall, Mardi Gras, 1872. City Hall was elaborately decorated for the visit of Grand Duke Alexis of Russia. A semicircular platform was erected at the front of the building, and its railings were trimmed with evergreens and small flags. In the center of the platform was erected a crimson canopy ornamented with gold fringe and lace. Flags of the United States, Russia, France, Prussia, and Britain, as well as the Confederate stars and bars, flew on either side of the entrance. An archway of gas jets with crystal shades topped the decorations. From this vantage point Alexis viewed the procession of Rex in the daytime and that of Comus that evening. From a sketch by G.M. in Frank Leslie's Illustrated Newspaper, March 9, 1872.

Carnival. After an interview with the mayor and the chief of police, who readily approved their ideas, a group was swiftly organized to finance the affair. Within thirteen days the five thousand dollars considered necessary to bring the organization into being was raised, and the plans for the first Rex parade were on their way. There was necessity for haste—the Grand Duke Alexis of Russia and his party were due to arrive in New Orleans in less than two weeks and apparently no plans had been made to entertain the distinguished visitors.

In 1872 Mardi Gras was not a legal holiday, but Rex, through a series of tongue-in-cheek royal edicts, called for a half-holiday and the closing of the schools, the post office, and the custom house; he even called on the Louisiana Lottery Company, then doing a land-office business, to desist from "any business whatever connected with the lottery on the day consecrated to His Majesty's reign." These edicts were probably the work of Hancock, a man of "wit, ingenious mind and fluent pen." They were written in a peculiar vein of solemn jocularity that made all of His Majesty's utterances and doings a travesty of monarchical usage so closely resembling the real thing and so delicately humorous that a universal popularity was at once established. The Rex organization, the

Working feverishly, the first Rex and his krewe laid plans for a gigantic Mardi Gras celebration. A carnival flag was designed in which a diagonal bar of gold ran from upper left to lower right forming an upper triangle (green) and a lower triangle (purple) with the crown of Rex in the center. Lithograph published by J. Curtis Waldo, ca. 1880.

School of Design, also created a royal flag, which has become traditional, consisting of a diagonal bar of gold from upper left to lower right forming two triangles; the upper triangle is green, and the lower is purple with a crown in the center of the golden bar. One interpretation is that royalty was represented by the purple, purity by the gold, and love and friendship by the green. However, in the Rex parade of 1892 with the theme "Symbolism of Colors," purple was identified with justice, green with faith, and gold with power. One of Rex's original edicts commanded that houses and places of business be decorated with bunting in carnival colors, starting another tradition that continues today. The king and the queen are presented with a special royal flag, which they are entitled to fly from their homes every Mardi Gras.

Alexis had arrived the day before Mardi Gras on the palatial Mississippi River steamer *James Howard,* and on the great day, after being formally received at City Hall by Governor Warmoth, Mayor B. F. Flanders, and General James Longstreet, he somewhat woodenly reviewed the first Rex parade. This mile-long spectacle was preceded by guns of a local artillery unit. These were followed by a white-bearded Rex who—clad in a purple silk velvet costume generously lent by the actor Lawrence Barret, who was then playing at the Varieties Theatre—rode a bay charger; the *boeuf gras,* alias Old Jeff, the decoy bull of the local stockyards; the Pack, maskers representing the fifty-two playing cards in the deck; and some five thousand maskers on foot and in wagons and in carriages. Interspersed were a number of bands, which had been commanded to play the official Mardi Gras tune, "If Ever I Cease to Love."

It had come to the ears of the Rex organization that Alexis had heard the popular Lydia Thompson sing "If Ever I Cease to Love" in the burlesque *Bluebeard* and had liked it. By a happy coincidence, she was then playing in New Orleans at the Academy of Music, and the tune was transposed into march time and dedicated to the grand duke. The catchy music with its numerous choruses

> If ever I cease to love,
> May oysters have legs and cows lay eggs. . . .
> May little dogs wag their tails in front,
> If ever I cease to love.

has ever since been the anthem of Rex, King of Carnival.

For the first time at a New Orleans Mardi Gras, the unorganized little groups of maskers had been organized into one parade, and it had been a tremendous success. Rex had great plans for 1873—he would have a

The 1874 Rex was banker William S. Pike, one of the founders of the School of Design. His queen was Margaret Maginnis. Pike, it was said, was slated to become the first Rex in 1872 but passed up the opportunity because he was fearful of riding a horse at the head of the newly organized group. By 1874 he had overcome his fears and rode at the head of the parade.

In 1895 Frank T. Howard, philanthropist, reigned as Rex, King of Carnival.

This regal figure in an ermine robe is Rex of 1901, Alfred Hennen Morris.

The styles of the king's dress change with the times. This Rex of 1896 is Charles Janvier.

grand ball primarily for the entertainment of visitors. Traditionally, the existing carnival krewes held exclusive balls, to which the visitors coming to New Orleans at carnival time in ever-increasing numbers were unable to get invitations. In 1873 Rex issued four thousand invitations to his first grand ball held at Exposition Hall on Mardi Gras night.

The ballroom was crowded at an early hour, and Rex, preceded by his court, marched in glittering procession twice around the hall. His Majesty, casting his eyes over the assemblage to choose a queen, halted before a lady he found most comely, Mrs. Walker Fearn. Taken completely by surprise, Mrs. Fearn (who had come to the ball out of curiosity

The first Queen of Carnival, 1873, was Mrs. Walker Fearn. The ballroom was crowded, and Rex, preceded by his court, marched in glittering procession twice around the hall. His Majesty, casting his eyes over the assemblage to choose a queen, halted before Mrs. Fearn. She had come to the ball out of curiosity and had on her second-best black dress, with a bonnet fastened under her chin, but she rose to the occasion, tossed her bonnet to her husband, and was crowned Rex's consort, the first Queen of Carnival.

and who had on her second-best dress) rose to the occasion, tossed her bonnet to her soldier-diplomat husband, and was thereupon crowned Rex's consort, the first Queen of Carnival.

In 1872 the Knights of Momus, organized along the same lines as Comus, held their first parade. Five years later in 1877, during the dying days of Reconstruction when Louisiana had two legislatures and two governors because of election frauds and New Orleans was in a sea of political corruption, Momus and his knights staged a pageant entitled "Hades, a Dream of Momus." The parade got off to a bad start when it was found that the float builders had neglected to measure the exit of the den in which the pageant had been constructed and some bricks had to be knocked out to permit the passage of the floats. Like the parade of Comus four years before, this one was a travesty on the political situation that, in Louisiana and in the United States, had reached an all-time low. The nineteen floats, depicting monsters, snakes, dragons, and infernal scenes like the abyss of fire and the furnace of Moloch, carried demoniacal forms whose countenances resembled those of such public

The early carnival balls were enlivened by tableaux. The third Momus ball (1876) had the subject "Louisiana and Her Seasons." There were three tableaux—Winter and Spring, with staples and flowers; Summer and Autumn, vegetables and fruits; and Momus receiving the Seasons, the grand finale of the previous tableaux with a white-bearded Momus sitting in its center.

figures as Hamilton Fish, James G. Blaine, Simon Cameron, Generals P. H. Sheridan and W. T. Sherman, and former governors Henry Clay Warmoth, William Pitt Kellogg, J. Madison Wells, and S. B. Packard. On the seventh car, high on the throne of Beelzebub, which was surrounded by Ethiopian monsters, sat "the grey-eyed man with the cigar," President Grant.

Immediate and violent reactions came from federal officials in New Orleans, who were infuriated at the deep political satire and who demanded punishment for the "outrage." Coming shortly after the disputed presidential election of 1876, the incident created considerable concern among the Louisiana Democrats, who had just installed the former Confederate general Francis T. Nicholls as governor in opposition to the Republican claimant S. B. Packard. Fearing repercussions, Nicholls wired an apology to Colonel E. A. Burke, the Louisiana intermediary in Washington. Fortunately, the affair quickly simmered down, and soon afterward Reconstruction ended.

KEEPERS OF THE CASH.

This float was a takeoff on the Freedmen's Bank. The trusting Negro at the top of the hill drops his savings into an iron safe with no bottom. Two characters, O. O. Howard and financier Jay Cooke, catch the money in a net. "Hades, a Dream of Momus," was the theme of the 1878 parade. From a parade paper.

Retired Veterans: Climbing the granite steps of the New Orleans Custom House are Governors Warmoth and Kellogg and the Radical figures Chamberlain and Moses of South Carolina, Adelbert R. Ames of Mississippi, and Bullock of Georgia. They are on their way to the Pension Agency in that building. This float appeared in the 1878 parade, "Hades, a Dream of Momus."

The Bloody Shirt float portrayed a great rock overhanging a pit of fire, the chasm of sectional hate. The figure represents Satan, described as Indiana Senator Oliver P. Morton who was noted for his waving of the "bloody shirt" in Congress. "Hades, a Dream of Momus" was the subject of the 1878 parade.

Another despised figure of the day, General Orville E. Babcock, rode on a float with vats representing a distillery. The float was further ornamented with imps and vipers. The subject of the 1878 parade was "Hades, a Dream of Momus."

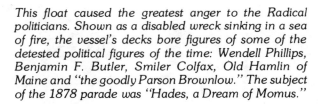

This float caused the greatest anger to the Radical politicians. Shown as a disabled wreck sinking in a sea of fire, the vessel's decks bore figures of some of the detested political figures of the time: Wendell Phillips, Benjamin F. Butler, Smiler Colfax, Old Hamlin of Maine and "the goodly Parson Brownlow." The subject of the 1878 parade was "Hades, a Dream of Momus."

Almost from the first, invitations to carnival balls were elaborate, exotic, and exquisite creations, lithographed in several colors and gold. Since the spirit of carnival has always been to have fun, the early invitations were amusing treasures to keep, royal memorabilia to pass through the ages, particularly as they often portrayed the theme of the ball, and the themes were, to put it mildly, ambitious.

The first Mardi Gras invitations were issued by the Mystick Krewe of

23

FRENCH OPERA HOUSE,
FRIDAY, FEBRUARY 14TH 1896.

STRICTLY PERSONAL.

M

COSTUME DE RIGUEUR.

1955

The Prophets of Persia

24

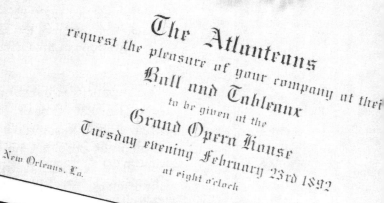

The Atlanteans
request the pleasure of your company at their
Ball and Tableaux
to be given at the
Grand Opera House
Tuesday evening February 23rd 1892
at eight o'clock

New Orleans, La.

Olympians
1911
French Opera House
Febru...

25

Comus, and the demand for them was far greater than the supply. In 1859, just two years after Comus was founded, the *Daily Picayune* commented, "Men go about, taking as much pains to secure an invitation to the great ball, as if they were electioneering for some fat office; supplications, introductions, recommendations, all are put in motion, and even bribery would be attempted if it could affect the thing. But it is all of no avail." So great was the desire to attend of some persons not invited to the 1860 Comus ball that, when they were denied entrance, they cried, "Fire," hoping in the confusion to get in. Colonel James McCloskey and General P. G. T. Beauregard, among the gentlemen standing near the entrance, helped restore order. In 1869 a number of uninvited ladies actually formed themselves into a flying wedge and tried to push their way in. Six crashers fainted, and others had their clothes torn.

From the outset the names of those to be invited have been approved by a secret committee with the absolute power to withhold invitations from those who in its judgment do not qualify for the honor. Each invitation to any of the carnival balls is strictly personal, and the admit card can only be used by the person to whom it is issued. When two invitations to the ball of the Mystick Krewe were stolen or lost in 1877, the *Daily Picayune* carried this advertisement:

REWARD—$2,000!
Whereas, two invitations to my festival, each numbered 22, have been stolen by some disloyal subject, now, therefore, be it known that a reward of $1,000 each will be paid by the keeper of my private purse for the return of the same to custodian of our royal archives.
This done in the twentieth year of our reign, Anno Domini, 1877.
COMUS

The reward was unclaimed; the invitations went unused.

The custom of presenting gifts to ladies "called out" by maskers at the balls is long standing, its origins lost in the mists of time. These favors, sometimes provided by the krewe with the insignia of the organization engraved or marked on them and sometimes bought by the maskers themselves, are presented to the ladies with whom they dance. The call-out section at the balls held in the Municipal Auditorium consists of the choicest seats at the rear of the parquet. The custom of call-outs (a masker asking through the intermediary of a committeeman for the lady chosen for the dance) originated in 1893 at the Proteus ball at the old French Opera House.

One of the strongest traditions of carnival is that of secrecy. This was especially true in the nineteenth century, when expulsion from the krewe was the penalty in some organizations for lifting one's mask or divulging secrets.

The first carnival organizations were exclusive clubs (and still are). They have been run primarily for the members and their friends, and invitations to their balls were and are sought after. Each year the carnival season attracted many visitors to New Orleans, and, though they could view the parades, it was almost impossible for the out-of-towners to get invitations to the balls. To remedy this situation the School of Design created its motto Pro Bono Publico, "for the public good," and made its invitations available to whomever would come attired in the proper raiment for attending a ball. In the past decade, however, Rex invitations are much more difficult to come by although, unlike the other organizations, all participants are invited to dance after the tableau, grand march, and first dance of the members and their ladies.

The Rex invitation of 1875, a masterpiece of color lithography, opened the glittering age of carnival ball invitations. Strangely enough, the School of Design had issued plain, simple invitations with engraved script in French to the first balls. One wonders which forgotten spirit in the organization originated the idea of having the invitations express the spirit of Mardi Gras and suggest the themes of the balls, and to do so in such colorful renditions. In the 1870s and 1880s the manager of the School of Design made annual trips to Paris to order costumes, jewelry, masks, and invitations. Some of the invitations, strikingly beautiful, consisted of as many as five parts bound in the shape of a book or formed to make a fan

Unpacking crates containing paper-mâché figures for the 1880 carnival. In the early years Rex annually sent a representative to Paris to contract for costumes, jewels, masks and figures for the floats. The deadpan masks still used today are made in France but the costumes and floats are created in New Orleans. From America Revisited, *by George Augustus Sala, London, 1886.*

or a bell or, in one instance, fastened as shields on a Viking ship. Others were cut in various shapes, lithographed in colors and gold, and cleverly designed to be unfolded. They reflected the opulence of the balls, the glittering costumes, the beauty of the queens, and the romance of the make-believe royalty. In contrast to the usual decorum of social mores, they were the very essence of the spirit of carnival, as if their designers and printers were enchanted by the task at hand.

Enclosed with the invitation would be an admit card. The dance

Rex ducal decorations, minor works of the jeweler's art in the 1880s and 1890s, were made in Paris. Even now the Rex decorations worn by its members are made in Europe. Shown are the ducal decorations for 1888 and 1892.

"The Missing Links" was the first parade to be constructed in New Orleans. Previously, the big masks and animal figures had been made in France, but by 1873 local artisans were able to make them stronger and no doubt cheaper. The illustration shows the interior of a den, where carnival masks and costumes are being prepared for the 1880 Mardi Gras. Sketch from America Revisited *by George Augustus Sala, London, 1886.*

programs then in vogue were created to match the invitations and were printed in similar colors and die cut in unusual shapes. In the early days the invitations to the tableau balls were delivered by special messenger. Uniformed officers of Boylan's Detective Agency and messengers from the telegraph companies were also used for this purpose. Later, delivery by messengers was superseded by the regular post.

Beginning in the late 1890s, Rex invitations were accompanied by souvenirs. These small metal objects—inkwells, letter openers, bonbon dishes, vases, etc.—were highly prized and sought by many even if they did not intend to attend the ball. In 1903 this krewe distributed twelve thousand of these souvenirs with the invitations. This custom ended with World War I.

Rex was followed in issuing colorful invitations in the 1880s by Comus, Proteus, Momus, and later Nereus and the Atlanteans, all vying to produce elaborate invitations, many of them in full color. Those of Comus, issued around the turn of the century when the art nouveau style was in vogue, are particularly striking.

A jewel box used as a Rex favor, 1907. These metal objects were sent with invitations to the Rex ball and are collectors' items today.

Promiscuous maskers on Canal Street. This is the way the artist B. West Clinedinst sketched the scene for Frank Leslie's Illustrated Newspaper *in 1893.*

In 1902, after issuing colorful folding and multicolored invitations for more than a quarter of a century, Rex discontinued the custom. Instead, a simple and dignified card designed and produced locally was introduced. The other krewes, however, continued to use elaborate invitations for many years. The custom of fancy ball invitations has been revived during the past few years, but the modern product only slightly resembles that of the 1880s and 1890s and is a dim echo of the flamboyant and joyous invitations of the past. Today most are in engraved script or dignified typography.

Dance program.

The subject of the 1882 Momus parade was the Ramayana. For the occasion Momus published an illustrated book of verses on this romantic tale of India. From a parade paper.

This was one of the floats in the Momus parade of 1884. The subject of the pageant was "The Passions" with floats representing Cruelty, Envy, Hate, Ambition, etc. From a parade paper.

Encouraged by the enthusiastic reception given their first efforts, Comus and his krewe produced an even better parade the next year, having the theme "The Classic Pantheon." There were thirty-one floats, on which rode maskers dressed to represent such characters as Jupiter, Minerva, Apollo, Janus, Ceres, Flora, Pan, and Bacchus. This pageant, which reportedly cost the members $20,000, was described by even the far-off London Illustrated News on May 8, 1858.

Carnival, 1883, seen through an artist's eyes. From Harper's Illustrated Weekly, *February 24, 1883.*

BEAUTIFUL SNOW

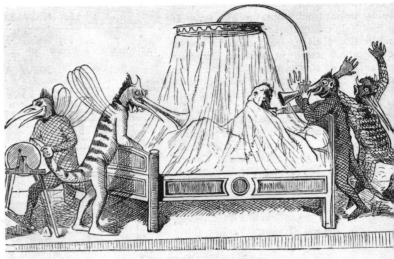

VOICES OF THE NIGHT

In the early 1880s two more organizations were born. The Independent Order of the Moon was founded by a group of funmakers whose purposes were similar to those of the Phunny Phorty Phellows and who cavorted on Mardi Gras each year until 1888 with floats ridiculing practically everything. Their theme for 1883 was "Familiar Rhymes Literally Interpreted."

MISSISSIPPI IN FLOOD

THE PÆAN OF THE BELLS

The first black-and-white pictures of the individual cars making up a carnival parade appeared in the late 1870s in the *Weekly Budget.* By the 1880s several New Orleans newspapers issued "parade papers," which were lithographed in color by a local firm and were sold on the streets for a dime, folded and ready to mail. Elaborate booklets—such as the ninety-four-page souvenir of Momus entitled *The Ramayana, the Iliad of the East,* a flowery book of verse illustrated by sixteen lithographs of the floats of the 1882 parade, or the hundred-page handsomely bound and illustrated book *Scenes from the Metamorphosis of Ovid* issued in 1878 by Comus to describe the scenes from that year's pageant—were published occasionally.

In the leading carnival organizations, men were the social arbiters. Working in secrecy, they devised the themes of tableau and pageant, passed on the names of those to be invited to the ball, and selected one of their members to be king, generally chosing his queen and her attendants as well. The work fell upon the captain of the krewe and his lieutenants, who assumed full responsibility for the success of the parade and the ball.

Starting in 1876, Rex began to "arrive" in his carnival capital on the Monday before Mardi Gras, usually by water, after an elaborate buildup

Frank B. Williams, Rex in 1909, has just presented his queen, Edith Libby, with a bouquet at the Boston Club. The docile crowd is lined against the curb in contrast to the behavior of crowds in the 1970s, which swarm all over the street.

The arrival of Rex on the Monday before Mardi Gras was inaugurated in 1874. This old print from Frank Leslie's Illustrated Newspaper *shows* Rex's arrival by the steamer Robert E. Lee for the 1879 carnival.

1904 Rex admission card advised holder to come in formal attire.

Prior to World War I, the arrival of Rex on his royal yacht Stranger at noon on the Monday before Mardi Gras was an aquatic spectacle viewed by thousands along the shores of the Mississippi. There was generally a visiting United States warship in the harbor and the vessels, from tugs to merchantmen, flew flags and tooted their whistles to honor the arrival of the King of Carnival.

Crowds waiting to greet Rex in 1908.

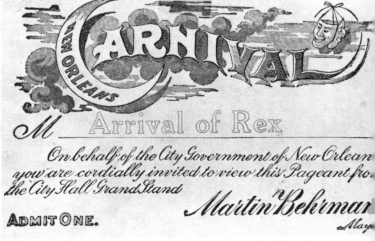

Rex was received at City Hall by the mayor on the Monday before Mardi Gras after arriving from his mythical kingdom. This is a complimentary invitation to view the proceedings from the steps of the City Hall, ca. 1914.

The arrival of Rex on the riverfront in 1906. Actually, another member of the organization impersonated Rex on the Monday before Mardi Gras. Those accompanying His Majesty are Colonel George Soulé, William Murray, Judge Albert G. Brice, and Morris Newman (wearing top hats). Members of the krewe, costumed and masked, followed.

Rex, King of Carnival, after arriving on the yacht Stranger at the foot of Canal Street, waits in his royal chariot to begin the parade in 1907.

Rex parade, 1907, at City Hall.

in the newspapers describing the trip from his mythical kingdom. In 1879 he arrived at the levee on the steamer *Robert E. Lee,* was met by a welcoming committee, and was escorted through the streets by a military contingent. This started a custom much enjoyed by the populace, that of "seeing the King come in." The flag-bedecked boats and ships in the harbor would form a water pageant of welcome, and Rex would arrive amid the booming of cannon and chorus of steam whistles. This custom lasted until 1917. It was revived in 1971 on the hundredth anniversary of the School of Design for one time only.

Another Rex tradition was the parading of the *boeuf gras* or fatted ox. In the Middle Ages, the *boeuf gras,* decked in ribbons and flowers and attended by butchers and cooks, was the symbol of Fat Tuesday.

In the third parade in 1874, Rex, as Totila, wore chain armor and rode on a horse. It was not until the fourth parade in 1875 that Rex rode in "a royal car, drawn by six white horses." Sketch by J. Wells Champney.

The garlanded, live boeuf gras *(fatted ox) was marched through the streets in the second Rex parade in 1873. Sketch by J. Wells Champney from* Scribner's Monthly, *December, 1873.*

The handsome beast, integral to every Mardi Gras celebration, was paraded year after year and represented the last meat to be eaten before Lent began on Ash Wednesday. The *boeuf gras* had appeared on the streets of New Orleans in the haphazard street festivities of the day for years before Rex came into being. In 1872, the *boeuf gras* held a featured spot in the first pageant of the King of Carnival and continued to parade ahead of His Majesty's float until 1901, when the custom was discontinued as "not in harmony with the beautiful displays which are produced in this era." It was not until 1959 that the *boeuf gras*—this time and in succeeding years a papier-mâché ox instead of a live one—reappeared in Rex pageants.

The subject of the 1896 Rex parade was "Planets, Stars, and Other Celestial Masses." The float illustrated was entitled "Argo Navis," and four of its five maskers sported beards.

Rex, 1885, passes on Canal Street to the applause of the crowds. At the ball on Mardi Gras night, some twenty thousand guests, it is said, paid homage to Rex and his consort. From Harper's Illustrated Weekly.

Part of the Rex parade of 1880 as sketched by George Augustus Sala, an English traveler who spent the carnival season in New Orleans that year.

The first three Rex parades were led by the king mounted upon a horse and followed by heterogeneous groups. It was not until the fourth pageant of maskers in carriages and on foot that Rex rode on a royal car and not until the fifth in 1876 that a full-blown formal parade of 25 floats depicting an ambitious theme, ''Military Progress of the World,'' was put on. This established a tradition that still exists after 91 Rex pageants and 1,807 Rex floats have paraded through New Orleans streets.

By throwing peanuts and candy to the outstretched hands of parade viewers in 1881, Rex's knights aboard the carnival floats reinstated the custom of the 1840s. This persisting custom now involves throwing literally tons of beads and cheap trinkets to the crowds. Several incidents come to mind. The first is a well-substantiated tale of a woman who, throwing an egg from one of the stands of a prominent club, hit the king of one of the night parades. Apparently she didn't like the king in real life and took this way to humiliate him. The other tale concerns the tossing of a bag of horse manure at one of the city leaders in front of Gallier Hall. This story has not been completely substantiated, but, even if true, who can blame a citizen for venting his spleen at a politician he doesn't like? When one considers the enormous crowds who have come to see the parades, a few untoward incidents only accentuate the good behavior of most of the viewers.

Rex has had many memorable moments since his inaugural appearance, but it is doubtful whether any parade was more unforgettable than that of Mardi Gras, February 14, 1899. A blizzard, which swept eastward out of the Rockies, deposited upon New Orleans three inches of snow, making the streets so hazardous that Proteus postponed his parade until the following Friday. When Walter D. Denegre, the Rex of the year, awakened that day, the temperature in New Orleans stood at 6.8 degrees, and a bitterly cold wind was sweeping the streets. His Majesty may have shuddered, but flinch he did not. And, although the carnival king was late in taking the streets, take them he did. The crowd was sparse in the subfreezing 28 degrees that prevailed during the parade. Rex made a valiant effort to be gay and to smile, but it was an icy smile for, so legend says, His Majesty's mustache had frozen. That night, under warmer conditions, Rex presided at the carnival palace with his queen, Perrine Kilpatrick.

In the early 1880s two more organizations were born. The Independent Order of the Moon was founded by a group of funmakers whose purposes were similar to those of the Phunny Phorty Phellows and who cavorted on Mardi Gras each year until 1888 with floats ridiculing practi-

The Phunny Phorty Phellows parade, 1896. The subject was "Popular Phads and Phancies." From a parade paper of the time.

A group of the members of Mississippi Fire Company No. 2 formed a new carnival club in 1878, the Phunny Phorty Phellows. When the older krewes paraded with mythological subjects, the Phellows took more earthy themes. For years their parades, designed for plain fun, were awaited with great eagerness by thousands who crowded the streets of New Orleans to watch.

French Opera House, scene of many carnival balls until it burned in 1919.

cally everything. In 1882 the Krewe of Proteus was organized by a group of young men from the New Orleans Cotton Exchange who used Comus, Momus, and the Twelfth Night Revelers as models. The Twelfth Night Revelers started the custom of choosing a queen in 1871. Rex followed in 1873, Momus in 1881, and Proteus in 1882.

At the carnival in 1882 Rex and his queen paid their first official visit to the court of Comus, who at that time ruled without a queen. This custom, the meeting of the courts of Rex and Comus, has since been the brilliant climax of Mardi Gras. The Comus ball of 1884 was especially memorable; at it the daughters of Jefferson Davis and Generals A. P. Hill, Robert E. Lee, and Stonewall Jackson were the honored guests. Comus called out Mildred Lee after the tableau, and the dukes danced the first quadrille with Varina Davis, Annie Hill, Julia Jackson, and Mary Lee. Although they were not designated so at that time, these daughters of the Confederacy were considered Comus' first court and Mildred Lee his first queen.

In 1892 Winnie Davis, another daughter of Jefferson Davis, was

The Rex ball of 1879. Bearded gentlemen in full dress and ladies in gowns with bustles and long trains stroll about Washington Artillery Hall, which had been decorated with flags and featured a garden centerpiece. The king and queen are on a raised dais in the rear center.

chosen queen of Comus. The theme of the parade and ball was "Nippon, the Land of the Rising Sun," and the Japanese costumes for the entire cast, as well as the royal jewels, were provided by the organization. The costume, scepter, and jewelry worn by Miss Davis have been preserved and are displayed at the Confederate Museum on Camp Street.

The use of electricity for lighting came to New Orleans in the late 1880s; in 1889 the Edison Company inspired the Knights of Electra to design a parade to demonstrate the incandescent lamp. A 12,000-pound steam generator mounted on a float and drawn by 16 mules supplied the power, which was conveyed through wires hidden in ropes to light the globes on the helmets of 128 participants, who were to march to "exemplify the practicability of electricity as an illuminator of moving bodies like processions." Unfortunately, the parade was rained out; a second postponement because of boiler trouble caused the thousands who had come to see the spectacle great disappointment; a third attempt suffered from lack of participants, who had heard a rumor that they might receive a fatal shock from the wires. Electricity did not again play a part in the parades until the Krewe of Nereus in 1900 mounted its pageant on regulation electric trolley trucks to portray "The Christian Era." There were delays, and the electric cars became separated; the incongruity of the trolley poles sticking up through the decorations of the floats caused widespread disapproval. Nereus retired thereafter from public parades and has since staged only tableau balls.

The Knights of Electra parade of 1889 marched to popularize the incandescent lamp.

Waiting for the parade. This was Canal Street in 1880. The spire of Christ Church on Canal and Dauphine is visible to the left, and horse-drawn cars and carriages were the order of the day. From America Revisited *by George Augustus Sala, London, 1886.*

BAND CAR.

The statue of Henry Clay (1873) (opposite page), located at the center of Canal Street at its intersection with St. Charles Avenue, was the rallying point for Mardi Gras merrymakers until removed to Lafayette Square in 1900.

The band car of the electrified parade of Nereus in 1900, which featured floats mounted on streetcars. One of the spectators, then a boy of seven, wrote many years later, "I thought the parade was pretty good. I distinctly remember the last car. It was one of the 'watering cars' [a large wooden tank mounted on a streetcar chassis] which were used to lay the dust in the streets during the summertime. It was all dolled up and it bore an illuminated sign, 'Jupiter Pluvius.'"

In 1890 an exciting episode occurred during carnival. Because the Mystick Krewe of Comus had not paraded or held a ball from 1884 through 1889, the Krewe of Proteus had taken its place for the night parade of Mardi Gras and for the ball at the opera. When Comus decided to return and take back his old evening, Proteus refused to resign. Perry Young in *Carnival and Mardi Gras* sets the stage: ''Both prepared their Mardi Gras parades and both went rolling at the same dark hour in towering, flashing, scintillating palaces, twenty-thousand dollars worth on either side. Proteus got there first and was blaring through the uptown strip of Canal Street as Comus blared out its downtown way.'' The result was that when Proteus, having circled Canal Street, turned to go down Bourbon Street to the French Opera House, the Comus parade, enroute to the Grand Opera House on Canal Street, blocked the crossing. Hot words and menacing gestures were exchanged by the Creole captain of Proteus and the Irish captain of Comus. The Proteus captain angrily declared that he would lead his parade through the Comus procession, cutting it in half. ''Over my dead body,'' roared the Comus captain. At that point a masker from the crowd—he was the brother of the Comus captain and a member of both Comus and Proteus organizations who

Rex took for the subject of his parade in 1879 the ambitious "History of the World," a comic travesty. The float shown is the Garden of Eden with Noah's Ark following. The parade was sketched at Canal and Royal streets.

had anticipated trouble—led the Proteus captain's horse away until the Comus parade had cleared the intersection.

Further complications ensued that night. On whom was Rex to call first? The matter had been discussed by the trustees of the Rex organization, and they had decided that His Majesty should call on Proteus first. But Rex himself had other ideas since he felt that Comus' carnival primacy entitled that monarch to be the first recipient of the King of Carnival's compliments. And so it was that Rex and his queen first visited the Grand Opera House, where they were greeted with a fanfare of trumpets and led to the throne with the orchestra playing the traditional "Triumphal March" from Verdi's *Aida.* After an appropriate interval they departed for the French Opera House. On their arrival the captain of Proteus failed to receive Rex and his consort; they were given a glass of champagne, after which their party, thus snubbed, left for the Pickwick Club. This social battle and the street confrontation of the two krewes was the sensation of the season and food for gossip to last through generations.

COOK.   BUTLER.   CARVER.   PASTRY COOK.

A feature of many early carnival parades and balls was the costuming, accessories, and masks of the members who participated. These caricatures were part of the 1878 "A Twelfth Night Revel" by the krewe of the same name. From a parade paper.

MACE-BEARER.   TWELFTH NIGHT CAKE

Then, as now, a feature of the Twelfth Night Revelers was the huge cake shown here carried by eight Revelers and preceded by the mace bearer. This engraving depicts a scene in the 1878 celebration. From a parade paper.

The Twelfth Night Revelers, which came into existence on Twelfth Night, January 6, 1870, was inaugurated by an eighteen-float street pageant. Its king, dubbed the Lord of Misrule (a term that is applied to Rex every now and then by the uninformed), was host at a tableau ball at the French Opera House. The main feature of this ball was a great cake in which a golden bean had been baked. The cake was cut and slices were distributed "with grace and courtesy by the maskers." Some of them passed the cake on their spears but, unfortunately, others "in their enthusiasm threw slices to ladies in the boxes. While this method of distribution created much merriment, the Golden Bean (whose fortunate finder was to be queen) was lost in the confusion and the Lord of Misrule was without a queen that year." The next year the Revelers were a little more systematic; they led their ladies to the cake and the Lord of Misrule himself cut the slices. The piece of cake containing the golden bean was drawn by the fortunate Miss Emma Butler, who then was crowned the first

queen of the Twelfth Night Revelers and incidentally the first queen of a carnival ball. The Twelfth Night Revelers, after several reorganizations in the century of its existence, no longer parades, but its carnival ball still features an immense decorated replica of a cake filled with small boxes containing slices of cake and the treasured bean. "Bakers" in white suits and tall bakers' hats assist the "head cook" who simulates the cutting of the cake with an immense knife. Another tradition of the Revelers is the plumed white feather that adorns the queen's crown.

The Knights of Momus notify those young women who will be in the court in time for them to have white dresses made for the occasion. The queen knows of her honor only when the chairman of the floor committee calls for her and presents the captain's scroll. At the ball she is crowned and arrayed in an elaborate mantle, and with her consort Momus, God of Mirth, she leads the grand march.

Momus, always known for liveliness and good-natured informality,

The last street parade of the Twelfth Night Revelers in 1878 was "A Twelfth Night Revel." Its members, disguised in papier-mâché masks and appropriate costumes, formed a tableau of a royal dinner at the theater. Here we see the Lord of Misrule, preceded by heralds and accompanied by characters disguised as musicians.

produced a tableau one year to commemorate the Louisiana Purchase. As part of the ceremony, the American flag was raised to the top of the flagstaff and a handful of soldiers in uniform (members of the organization) fired a salute with blank cartridges. Immediately—and doubtless on the initiative of some enterprising member of the cast—a dead duck fell from the heights, much to the edification and astonishment of the ladies and other guests present.

The Krewe of Consus, no longer in existence, created one sensational ball after another from 1897 to 1906. "Robin Hood and His Merry Men," the subject of the first ball on February 12, 1897, was the beginning of a series of dazzling tableaux. Particularly noteworthy was the 1898 ball, "The Meeting of King Henry VIII of England and Francis I of France on the Field of the Cloth of Gold," in which the boxes and tiers from the top to the bottom of the French Opera House were decorated with gold cloth and a gigantic golden spider web adorned the ceiling. Their third ball. "Salle des Glaces de Versailles" was especially brilliant. Using glass and mirrors, the Hall of Mirrors at Versailles was recreated. It was illuminated by electric lights and a myriad of gas-fueled candles; the mirrors, set at angles, caught and reflected images to infinity. Against this setting, members in appropriate costume formed rich tableaux. "The House Boat on the Styx" was Consus' next presentation. The cast came onto the stage to the dirge of Chopin's Funeral March and entered a

The first black-and-white pictures of the individual cars making up a carnival parade appeared in the late 1870s in the Weekly Budget. *In the 1880s several New Orleans newspapers issued "parade papers" lithographed in colors by a local firm and sold folded and ready to mail.*

Float No. 20, Germany, in the Rex parade on February 12, 1907. The theme was "Visions of Nations," and this float was ornamented with an armored knight, an imperial crown, crenelated castles, and the imperial German arms.

If one could not afford to buy a costume, mother could make one for you. Here we have two monkeys, complete with sawdust-stuffed tails, a Happy Hooligan, an Uncle Sam with a long nose, and three characters of uncertain ancestry. The time—about 1910.

A crowd waits for a parade, 1903.

banquet hall resplendent with thousands of jewellike ornaments. In 1901, Consus, whose reputation by this time was the clever shattering of traditions, put on "Shakespeare and His Creations" with a setting of real trees and flowers. Things went well for the next few years until 1906, when the presentation was "The Land of Frontinback and Upondown." This upside-down ball featured skies and clouds underfoot and trees and fields growing down from overhead. The fatal mistake was to have the cast walking and dancing apparently backward. This was accomplished by having double masks—one worn over the face that concealed the masker's features by representing the back of the head (with peepholes for eyes) and a false face that was worn over the back of the head. The costumes carried out the same idea. The effect during the tableau was comical, but, when the maskers began to dance, their ladies found their partners' backs turned on them. Aside from the physical impoliteness, which of course was only in appearance, the ladies who had before always danced the other way were highly displeased. After the ball, resignations quickly reduced Consus to the history books.

In former days most parades consisted of eighteen to twenty floats, including the title float and the king's throne car. The parades were designed by highly skilled carnival artists and built by trained artisans who created in wood, papier-mâché, cloth, paint, and gold and silver leaf the mythological, legendary, fanciful, satirical, or comical subjects chosen for

Mardi Gras fun in a Tin Lizzie, ca. 1915.

Four "dukes for a day" in carnival finery, ca. 1915.

Street maskers, such as these clowns and peasant girls, about 1916, were much more common on Mardi Gras before the advent of organized truck parties.

The same group shown at the bottom of this page, ensconsed in a hired barouche, sets out to see the sights.

Four masked, mysterious maids, ca. 1920. Note the Mardi Gras whips carried to ward off unwanted attentions.

Backyard Indian maid and suitor, Mardi Gras, 1915.

Mardi Gras maskers, some in borrowed navy and army uniforms, others in homemade outfits, pose for their picture one Mardi Gras around 1920. In the background is a lad who brandishes two empty beer bottles, the contents of which have no doubt helped the fun along.

Each Mardi Gras half a dozen marching clubs parade before the Rex parade. (One of these, the Jefferson City Buzzards, has paraded for more than eighty years.) Starting out in uptown New Orleans early on Mardi Gras and always accompanied by a band, the costumed members strut and sway their way through crowded streets. This is a marching club on Mardi Gras, 1925.

These two celebrants in black-face set out to see the sights and to be seen on Mardi Gras some time around 1920. The King of Portugal boasts a gilded top hat and carries a stick for a scepter. The Queen of Atlantic City, obviously a male, carries a parasol.

the spectacle. The floats of the first parades were drawn by horses, but later these were replaced by mules that, after humbly pulling the city's garbage wagons on other days, had three nights and a day of glory at carnival time. The night parades were illuminated by colorful flares and by flambeaux (gasoline reflector torches) carried by dancing Negroes. Marching bands of musicians, spaced between the floats, provided melody and foot-tapping rhythm. Carnival was, for the man in the street, the biggest free show in the world, and he loved it.

To Reuben H. Brown, King of Carnival in 1950, and his queen, Mary Brooks Soulé, came a unique honor denied all other kings and queens of carnival. The man who had been Edward VIII, the king of England, now the duke of Windsor, bowed to the Mardi Gras monarchs, and his duchess curtsied before the enthroned rulers of the carnival. During the parade, the duke and duchess of Windsor were the guests on the Boston Club gallery with the carnival queen and her court, and they returned the salute that Rex directed to them. *Life* magazine said that the duke and duchess had set New Orleans in a whirl when it had become known that they would attend carnival: "The New Orleans Mardi Gras, which has taken almost every conceivable happening in its stride for the

The once king of England, the duke of Windsor, and his duchess salute the onetime King of Carnival on Mardi Gras night, 1950.

past 123 years, was really set on its ear last week, when news came that the Duke and Duchess of Windsor were coming. Nobody worried that the Windsors would not enjoy the goings-on, but they all wondered what would happen when they were presented to the Carnival rulers. It is Mardi Gras custom for all gentlemen to bow and all ladies to curtsy when presented to the Mardi Gras Kings and Queens." The duke and duchess arrived early, watched the parade of Rex, had cocktails at Beauregard House, dinner at Antoine's, and finally, at ten o'clock arrived at the Municipal Auditorium. They were guided first to the Comus ball, then to the Rex ball, and at each they were complete conformists, the duke bowing low and the duchess dipping in a royal curtsy. New Orleans was bowled over. So apparently was the duchess. "Fabulous," she gasped, "and such fun."

The year 1960 was a momentous one for the School of Design and for carnival as well. During the reign of Gerald L. Andrus and his queen, Stella Evans Farwell, Rex's now famous doubloon, which took the crowd by storm and started a tradition, was tossed by the maskers for the first time. Years earlier, Rex had produced medallions similar to the doubloon on two occasions, in 1884 and 1893. This points up the famous comment of Madame Bertin, milliner of Marie Antoinette: "There is nothing new, except what is forgotten."

The idea for the Rex doubloon came from H. Alvin Sharpe, a retired ship captain and highly skilled designer and engraver, who addressed the following letter to the School of Design on December 5, 1959:

Sirs:

I would like to make *immediate* contact with someone in authority in your organization.

I have designed some very beautiful "Doubloons" that can be coined in soft aluminum (Gold or Bright) very cheaply.

I feel that these "Rex coins" would be a sensation as a memento of Mardi Gras. They are harmless to throw away.

I will need your *approval* and full cooperation if these coins are to be produced, and time is *very, very* short.

The Rex organization received many requests and offers of products, and it was only by accident that this letter was not tossed into the wastebasket. It struck the fancy of the Rex lieutenant charged with correspondence, who called it to the attention of the captain. Sharpe, invited to discuss the matter, presented his design and demonstrated how a light aluminum medallion could be thrown from the floats without injuring anyone. Impressed with the idea, the Rex captain immediately arranged to underwrite the first issue of the Rex doubloon. Alvin Sharpe went speedily to work to engrave the dies, strike off 83,000 doubloons, 80,000 in natural aluminum finish and 3,000 in gold anodized finish, and deliver them to the Rex den several weeks before Mardi Gras, which fell on March 1. Instant favor with the crowd was won. The traditional cry, "Hey mister, throw me something," became "Hey, mister, throw me a doubloon!"

The 1960 Rex doubloon has become a scarce item, much sought after by collectors. The natural-finish aluminum medallion, which cost the Rex members $.03 each, was cataloged in 1974 at $15 to $20. The scarcer anodized coin listed as high as $80 to $85. Even scarcer, with a much greater collector's price tag, was the anodized doubloon that the King of Carnival, Gerald Andrus, had hand-stamped with the date 1960, because the first issue of the Rex doubloon was undated. Only 330 of these were hand-stamped for His Majesty, and the medallion catalogs list them at about $150 each. Even higher is the value for the scant number of sterling silver 1960 Rex doubloons. Prices as high as $1,500 to $1,800 have been offered by collectors on the infrequent occasions when one of these rarities shows up. The popularity of the Rex doubloon has increased year by year. In 1974 the mintage totaled 500,000, bringing the 15-year total from 1960 to 1970 to more than 5,000,000.

In a short time, practically every carnival krewe created its own medallion to throw from the floats or use as a favor at the balls or both. Eventually the word *doubloon,* originally linked to Rex, became a generic term meaning any and all carnival medallions.

Until World War I, with but minor variations, the carnival schedule went this way: the parade and ball of Momus occurred on Thursday evening before Mardi Gras; amid pomp and ceremony Rex arrived on the levee at noon the Monday before; the Proteus parade and ball were held Monday evening; the parade of Rex and street masking of the people were during the day on Mardi Gras, followed by the evening parade of Comus and climaxed by the balls of Comus and Rex.

As the city grew, new organizations were formed to participate in the carnival celebration. In the last decade of the nineteenth century, seven new bodies appeared: Atlanteans (1891); Original Illinois Club (1894); Elves of Oberon (1895); Nereus (1896); High Priests of Mithras (1897); Les Mysterieuses (1896); and Consus (1897). From 1900 to 1919, twelve societies were formed: Falstaffians, Olympians, Mittens, Amphicytons, Zulu, Athenians, Nippon, Osiris, Mystery, Iris, Yami, and Artimissians. Thirteen appeared in the 1920s: Druids, Mystic, Harlequins, Prophets of Persia, Les Marionettes, Apollo, Carrollton, Children's Carnival Club, and Young Men's Illinois included among them.

It was in the 1930s and 1940s that the greatest numerical growth of carnival groups occurred. In the thirties there were nineteen new organizations: Bards of Bohemia, Mid-City, Arabi, Hypatians, Aporomest, Moslem, Eros, Omardz, Elenians, Caliphs of Cairo, Noblads, Hermes, Orpheus, Dorians, Sonians, Virgilians, Prometheus, Elks Krewe of Orleanians, and Alla. The forties witnessed the greatest growth in any

The 1934 Rex invitation was a simple card reflecting the austerity of the times.

"Plutocrats for a day," Mardi Gras, ca. 1915. This party with homemade full dress suits and hired top hats has engaged a carriage to take in the sights.

A Gallagher's furniture moving van ("The World Moves—So Does Gallagher") with the signs of the builders of the parade, Soulie & Crassons, brought up the rear of every Rex parade in former years, shown here in 1936. It was the property wagon, and on it rode some of the proud builders of the floats that had passed in parade.

A women's carnival parade of the 1930s. Note that the floats are pulled by men.

decade—twenty-five. They were: Babylon, Musica, Eurydice, Venus, Fantasy, Niobeans, Alhambra, Achaeans, Hera, Janus, Mokana, Cynthius, Carthage, Grela, Maids of Troy, Jefla, Theron, Pericles, Adonis, Thoth, Les Pierettes, Naiads, Hebe, Choctaw, and Caronis.

In 1950, Edward E. Soulé, a former King of Carnival, spoke to members of the Rex organization about the proliferating balls and parades:

> . . . No doubt you have all heard from many well-meaning but mistaken critics that we are going carnival crazy in New Orleans, with so many carnival balls and so many day and night parades of both men and women, it would seem no doubt to many of you that we should call a halt. . . . but New Orleans is now a city of more than 650,000 people, and every good citizen, like ourselves, is entitled to participate in the joys and pleasures and mysteries of a masked ball and a carnival parade. . . .
>
> . . . The older parade organizations have full membership. It is difficult to join any of them. The same situation prevails in many of the old tableaux balls. It follows then, that other organizations must provide for other pleasure-seekers like yourselves, and therefore the answer must be more organizations if necessary.

His words were prophetic; in the 1950s fourteen new organizations were founded; there were sixteen formed in the 1960s; and more than a score have sprung up in the 1970s.*

Since the advent of Comus, well over a hundred carnival organizations have been formed. Many of these languished; some were revived and after a few years passed from the scene to be followed by others that took their places. In the 1970s there have been usually more than fifty carnival parades and ninety balls each year in New Orleans and its suburbs. These newer groups encompass all types of organizations: some are organized and run by women; quite a few are organized by promoters; some are neighborhood groups; some are ethnic in origin. But all give almost any citizen with sufficient means the opportunity to join and even to become a king or queen!

Nick Lemann, writing in *New Orleans* magazine, tells some little-known facts about the krewes he terms the "elite." He estimates that, of all carnival krewes, the least reported on, most mysterious, and

---

*Krewes organized in the 1950s: Okeanos, Jupiter, Ball Masque, Orion, Sparta, Zeus, Pegasus, Helois, Helena, Midas, Cronus, Anubis, Ancient Scribes, and Freret. Krewes organized in the 1960s: Juno, Diana, Ulysses, Squires, Jason, Mecca, Endymion, Golden Age, Bacchus, Hercules, Nemesis, Arabi, Hebe, Gemini, Terpsichore, and Les Daneuses. Krewes organized in the 1970s: Rhea, Pan, Hesper, Iris, Atlas, Shangri-La, Gladiators, Nike, Daughters of Eve, Pandora, Vikings of Tyr, Artemis, Argus, Jefferson, Tucks, Capetowners, Jugs, Armor, Neophermenos, and Winnebago.

King of the Zulus (Alonzo Butler) is shown here in the 1940s (right); the Big Shot of Africa (center); and the Grand Marshal (left).

A Zulu with his bag of coconuts.

At one time prizes for the best maskers were given on Mardi Gras from a judges' stand on Canal Street by the Young Men's Business Club. This photograph, taken in the 1940s, has the Terminal Railroad Station in the background. Two diaper-clad males sporting baby caps brave the chilly weather to compete for a prize.

A Zulu tradition (opposite page) calls for the dispensing of coconuts, which the king tosses to friends and acquaintances along the parade route.

A dozen or so grass-skirted members of the Krewe of Zulu prepare for arrival from the tug Fox in the New Basin Canal one Mardi Gras morning in the 1930s. Zulu then mounted his royal float and, followed by a happy crowd of on-lookers, began his peripatetic journey about town.

hardest to join are Comus, Momus, Proteus, and Rex, all of which parade, and Atlanteans, Mystick, Twelfth Night, Oberon, and Mithras, which hold balls. All nine of these krewes are private, and their memberships are secret. They are made up of white Christian men only, except Rex, which does not bar Jews from membership.* All of the nine, except Mystick, were founded before 1900, and four of them have been in existence for more than a century. Most of the elite krewes have come in for considerable censure for their policy of barring Jews from membership and not inviting them to their balls. On the other hand, these krewes have barred a great many more local gentile aspirants to their organizations. They say that they are private clubs and that their policy is to invite whom they please.

But carnival and Mardi Gras are changing, and customs established years ago are being transformed. The Krewe of Bacchus, founded in 1968, initiated great changes in parade design and in its ball. Floats are larger than the conventional size to accommodate twenty riders instead of eight or ten. The designs are more elaborate, and the king is a celebrity in the entertainment field instead of a member of the organization. The ball is a huge supper-dance at the Rivergate, and the floats and their riders come right into the hall that holds the guests. Instead of invitations, tickets are sold for the affair. At one of the balls, to the writer's knowledge, black guests were seated at tables with their white counterparts.

Endymion, a krewe of just ordinary pretentions, suddenly in 1974 blossomed with a parade that possibly outdid the spectacular Bacchus pageant. Endymion paraded even its gaudily costumed maids, dukes, king, and queen on its floats! Some say that Bacchus and Endymion have made the other nighttime parades of Momus, Comus, and Proteus look old and tired. Even Rex, parading under the more difficult light of day, suffers by comparison, although the School of Design spends much money on its floats and costumes.

Another factor in a changing carnival is the proliferation of parades in the New Orleans suburbs. Of the fifty-seven processions mounted in 1975, twenty-four were held in New Orleans proper, and thirty-three marched in its suburbs—eleven in Metairie, seven in Gretna-Algiers, six in St. Bernard Parish, five in Chalmette-Arabi, three in Kenner, and one

---

*A number of present-day krewes have Jewish members. Another little-known fact is that in the 1890s and early 1900s there were two Jewish carnival clubs that held balls during the carnival season. They were the Harmony Club and the Young Men's Hebrew Association. Lacour writes, "Diminishing interest in activities at Carnival time resulted in the discontinuance of the Harmony Club Balls," and the Young Men's Hebrew Association balls soon followed suit.

in Harahan. No longer is it necessary to travel to downtown New Orleans to see a parade. The suburbs have their own pageants, some of which are just as splendid as those in the city. An additional factor is the massing of costumed Mardi Gras revelers on decorated floats (flatbed trucks) in parades following the Rex parade. The first was initiated by Chris Valley, who founded the Elks Krewe of Orleanians in 1935. The Krewe of Crescent City, organized by A. Russell Calogne in 1946, removed still more potential maskers from the scene. The result is that street masking, though not dead, is but a shadow of its former self. Perhaps the crowds have become just too dense for individuals in costumes to brave. Whatever the causes, Mardi Gras is turning into a spectator affair. But, with all its faults, today carnival is great fun for thousands of ball goers, and Mardi Gras is the ''greatest free show on earth'' for anyone who takes the time to be part of it.

White-caparisoned mules drew His Majesty's throne car until the coming of tractors after the 1949 carnival. Shown here is Rex toasting his queen at the Boston Club.

Mardi Gras, 1942 or 1943. It was wartime and Rex did not parade, but there was a float with a serviceman as king.

The Rex parade (opposite page) coming into Canal Street from St. Charles Avenue in 1953. This scene is repeated every year on Mardi Gras when the street is literally jammed with thousands of spectators.

Another colorful custom was the strutting of the Negro "Baby Dolls," who wore short skirts, pinafores, and sun-bonnets. Often tipsy from drink, they would go about in groups chanting in Creole patois over and over again, "Aye, aye, aye. Mo pé allé quitté" (Hey, hey, hey. I'm going to quit [my job]).

Rex parade, 1952, with the theme "Panorama Through the Magic Sugar Egg."

Osiris carnival ball, 1950s.

Truck parade, 1960s.

After an absence of fifty-eight years, the boeuf gras, *the ancient symbol of Mardi Gras, reappeared in the Rex parade of 1959. Each year since a papier-mâché boeuf gras has been featured in every Rex parade, as in 1962, shown here.*

Rex parade, 1960, with the theme "The Wonderful World of Let's Pretend."

Rex parade, 1964, with the theme "The Wizard of Oz."

Rex Parade, 1963. What would Mardi Gras be without the marching bands?

The Streetcar Named Desire joined Rex in 1968. With its jazz band on top, this jolly trolley has been a popular feature ever since.

Rex parade, 1972.

Rex parade, 1972, in front of the Pickwick Club.

The captain of the Rex parade, 1972.

The dance floor at a carnival ball is a wonderfully colorful scene. Shown here is the 1974 ball of the Krewe of Osiris.

Rex parade, 1965 (left and above), with the theme "Once Upon a Time."

A Mardi Gras day crowd on Canal Street in 1963. Each year on Mardi Gras more and more people crowd the streets to view the parades. From the traditional four of earlier years, there were some fifty parades scheduled in or near the city during the 1970s.

Rex, his queen, and his court in 1970.

Resplendent Comus holding the traditional cup poses with his dazzling queen at the Comus ball, February 18, 1969.

Some Mardi Gras participants display great originality. This gent with his wig and Indian belly rig was a crowd stopper on Mardi Gras, 1959.

Faust and Mephisto, 1959. Before World War II it was the custom of merchants near certain city markets to hold costume competitions that always attracted large crowds. Such a contest is held each year in the Vieux Carré; it attracts all types of contestants, many with bizarre costumes.

Pete Fountain's Half-Fast Marching Club, ca. 1971.

Costumed members of Pete Fountain's Half-Fast Marching Club, ca. 1970.

*Masked and costumed revelers take to the streets on
Fat Tuesday (this page through page 85).*

84

One of the floats of the revamped 1974 parade of the Krewe of Endymion. Note the relatively large size of the float.

Typical of the lavish floats of the Krewe of Bacchus is this one, the Bacchusaurus. Its great size may be judged by comparison with the crowd clamoring for doubloons, which were being thrown by handfuls by the krewe members in the barrels attached to the creature's sides.

King Bob Hope, the comedian, majestically rides the throne car in the 1973 parade of the Krewe of Bacchus.

The Elks Krewe of Orleanians was the brainchild of Chris Valley, a member of the New Orleans Lodge of Elks. Up to the 1930s many private groups hired trucks and rode about the city on Mardi Gras to see the sights. Some of these people were in costume, and some had decorated trucks. Valley conceived the idea of organizing the truck riders into a parade to follow the Rex parade. The first year there were 55 entries, but the trucks became separated. In 1936, however, better organized, the Elks parade became a reality, and it has grown to some 160 floats each year. Often executed with great skill, the floats carry as many as 6,000 costumed riders. The Krewe of Crescent City follows the Elks Krewe of Orleanians. Because both organizations had so many vehicles, the city authorities had to limit the number of floats in each. The elaborate floats of the Elks krewe often rival, and sometimes surpass, the floats of the great carnival organizations. Shown here is a float in the 1973 parade.

Half a dozen krewes have sprung up in the St. Bernard–Arabi neighborhoods in suburban New Orleans. Here we see the 1963 king of one of them, sans crown and scepter, toasting his queen.

Flambeaux and bearers at a night parade, 1950s.

The Boston Club in New Orleans is decorated with lights for the Krewe of Proteus.

89

The climax of carnival is the lavish spectacle of the meeting of the courts of Rex and Comus, here the 1964 meeting. Both krewes hold their balls on Mardi Gras night, and, in accordance with long-established custom, the captain of Comus comes to the Rex ball to extend an invitation to Rex to visit the Comus ball. A little before midnight Rex and his queen arrive at the ball of Comus, and the two glittering courts meet to the applause of the guests.

At the Rex ball, 1950, Reuben H. Brown and Mary Brooks Soulé were the carnival rulers.

Members of the Rex organization and their ladies approach the throne to bow and curtsy to the 1971 Rex and his queen. Unlike other carnival balls, only the captain and three of his lieutenants are in costume and masked; the members of Rex are in full dress and their ladies in ballroom finery. The first dance is for members and their wives; then the floor is opened to the guests.

Decorated truck in Elks Krewe of Orleanians parade.

Wall-to-wall people is the way that some observers have described Canal Street on Mardi Gras. Here shown are the first floats of a Rex parade in the 1950s surrounded by a sea of people.

A last quick glance at regal splendor—queen of an Osiris ball, scepter in hand, prepared to meet her king.

Leon Sarpy, who reigned as Rex, King of Carnival, in 1972, waves to the crowds on Canal Street.

Several times gigantic comic figures have paraded on Mardi Gras. These oversized clowns preceded the Rex parade in 1962. The theme of the pageant was "The Year of the Circus."

"The Owl and the Pussycat" cruising along Canal Street in Mardi Gras, 1965. The mules which formerly pulled the Rex floats have been replaced by tractors disguised as horses.

Photo Credits

Special Collections Department, Howard-Tilton Memorial Library, Tulane University—page 9 (right), 14 (top right), 20–21, 29, 31 (bottom), 32 (top), 49, 50–51.

Ray Cresson—6, 36 (left center), 64–65, 67, 69 (top left, bottom), 70 (bottom), 71 (center, bottom), 75 (top left), 79–85, 86 (top), 89 (bottom left), 92–93, 95.

Manuel C. DeLerno—17 (top left), 61 (bottom), 72 (bottom), 73–74, 76 (bottom), 86 (bottom), 87–88, 94.

John J. De Paul—54, 56, 57 (bottom), 61 (top).

Library of Congress—14 (left), 37 (bottom left and right).

Angela Gregory—58.

Edmond Souchon—37 (top).

Augusto P. Miceli—75 (bottom).

Adolph J. Claverie—77–78.

Louis Darré, Jr.—76 (top), 91.

Charles Geriella—62.

Charles L. Franck—57 (top).

Leonard V. Huber—2, 11–12, 17 (top right, bottom left and right), 19, 25, 28, 32 (bottom), 33, 35, 36 (bottom right), 38–39, 42, 46 (top), 47–48, 53, 55, 68, 69 (top left), 71 (top), 72 (top left and right), 89 (top, bottom right), 90.